MARTINEZ

D0633501

Where Does
Food
Come From?

To Gary who makes food fun — Shelley

To my mother whom I loved very dearly— even though she taught me that all foods came from a can! — Gary

Millbrook Press
A division of Lerner Publishing Group
241 First Avenue North
Minneapolis, Minnesota 55401 U.S.A.

Website address: www.lernerbooks.com

Library of Congress Cataloging-in-Publication Data

Rotner, Shelley.
Where does food come from? / by Shelley Rotner and Gary Goss.
p. cm.
ISBN-13: 978-0-7613-2935-0 (lib. bdg.:alk. paper)
ISBN-10: 0-7613-2935-8 (lib. bdg.:alk. paper)
1. Food industry and trade—Juvenile literature. I. Goss, Gary. II. Title.
TP370.3.R68 2006
664—dc22
2005000874

DESIGNED BY KATIE CRAIG

Manufactured in the United States of America
1 2 3 4 5 6 – JR – 11 10 09 08 07 06

Where Does Food Come From?

Shelley Rotner and Gary Goss
Photographs by Shelley Rotner

MILLBROOK PRESS · MINNEAPOLIS

Did you know?

A chocolate-candy maker is called a chocolatier....Fancy schmancy!

Cocoa beans

are seeds that grow on cocoa trees.

Chocolate

is made by grinding and cooking cocoa beans.

Hot cocoa

is made from chocolate.

Apples are fruits
that grow on trees.

An **apple** can be
eaten right off the tree!

Apple juice
is made by pressing the
juice from apples.

Did you know?

There are more than 7,000 different kinds of apples. What's your favorite kind?

Potatoes

are vegetables that grow under the ground.

French fries

are made by cutting up potatoes and then cooking them in hot oil.

Did you know?

President Thomas Jefferson is given credit for introducing french fries to America.

Did you know?

A freight train full of one year's wheat crop would stretch around the world two and a half times!

Wheat is a grain
that grows in fields.

Flour is often made
from ground-up wheat.

Bread is made
mostly from flour.

Did you know?

More than half the people in the world rely on rice as the main part of their meals.

Rice is a **grain** that grows in wet fields called paddies.

Rice that you eat is made by cooking the kernels of grain.

Did you know?

There are 16 rows of kernels on each and every ear of corn.

Corn is grain that grows on stalks in fields.

Cornstalks grow cobs that are covered with corn kernels.

Popcorn is made when kernels of corn are popped.

Did you know?

Cows drink a lot of water. It would be like a human drinking 500 glasses a day!

Milk comes from **cows** — or sometimes from goats.

Your milk is made safe for you to drink by first heating it and then keeping it cool in a bottle or carton.

Milk is the main ingredient in butter, cheese, and ice cream.

Lemons are citrus fruits that grow on trees.

Lemonade is made by adding water and sugar to the juice of lemons.

Did you know?

A lemon is a type of berry.

Did you know?

It takes most hens about a day to produce an egg.

The kind of eggs you eat are laid by domestic **hens**, birds that live on farms.

Scrambled is one way to serve **eggs**. People also like to eat eggs fried or poached or hard boiled.

Tomatoes

grow on vines.

Tomato sauce

is made by cooking tomatoes.

So is **ketchup**.

Did you know?

The largest tomato ever grown weighed more than 7 pounds.

Did you know?

Peanut butter was invented by a doctor for his elderly patients who couldn't chew. Later, because plain peanut butter on bread was so dry, jelly was added, to create a new and delicious sandwich.

Peanuts are beans that grow in the ground.

Peanut butter is made by grinding peanuts.

Grapes are fruits that grow in bunches on vines.

Grape jelly is made by cooking grapes.

Lettuce, tomatoes,
cucumbers, carrots,
and peppers can
all grow in gardens.

Salads are
made by combining
these and other
vegetables or fruits.

Did you know?

Cucumbers, peppers, and tomatoes are actually fruits because they have seeds inside.

Did you know?

The honeybee can beat its wings more than 200 times per second.

Honey is made by bees delivering the nectar of flowers to the hive.

Did you know?

It takes 40 gallons of sap to make 1 gallon of maple syrup.

Maple syrup is made by boiling the sap that comes from the maple tree.

Salt comes from seawater.

Did you know?

Salt is the only rock we eat.

Sugar comes from the juice of sugarcanes and also from sugar beets.

Did you know?

The average teenager eats 110 pounds of sugar a year, which is 13 tablespoons a day!

Where does *your* **favorite food** come from?